Heavenly Realm Publishing

*Houston, Texas*

ISBN—13: 9781937911- 55-3

Library of Congress Control Number: 2013911403
The Locker Room Experience: *For the Struggling Athlete & Coach, & Tips on How to Get Recruited in Sports*/ Stephanie Franklin

This book is printed on acid free paper.

Printed in the United States of America

**Published By: Heavenly Realm Publishing**
**P. O. Box 682532**
**Houston, TX 77268**
**www.heavenlyrealmpublishing.com**
**Toll Free 1-866-216-0696**

# The
# LOCKER
# ROOM

## *Experience*

### For the Struggling Athlete & Coach,
### & Tips on How to Get Recruited in Sports

*Middle School * High School * College * Pro Athlete & Coach*

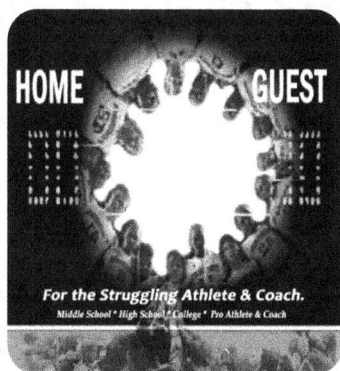

HOME     GUEST

**For the Struggling Athlete & Coach.**
Middle School * High School * College * Pro Athlete & Coach

# Stephanie Franklin

*For every person, athlete and coach desiring,*
*seeking and inspiring to get better and win.*


*For every athlete who desires to get*
*recruited into college or pro.*

# THE **LOCKER ROOM** *Experience*
## Introduction

With over twenty years of experience in the sporting arena and fifteen in the education arena, I have had the opportunity and experience of teaching (*educating*), helping, mentoring, rehabilitating, training and coaching many athletes and students to promising careers and futures. One became a professional basketball player (Kendrick Perkins plays for the Oklahoma Thunder), others received college scholarships, academic scholarships, colleges and top university acceptances, and trade and industrial schools acceptances. I have also helped little league athletes to become strong through mentorship (physical, health, mental, and emotional growth training, coaching and rehabilitation). I have had the opportunity to coach little league baseball players through my Strength Training, Rehabilitation, and Off-Season Program; while at the same time helping them find their potential and purpose in the art of life and athletics. Through this experience, I have also seen many athletes miss out on rewarding futures of being able to pursue the sport they are well qualified in, and able to excel at, because they lack the help they need to push them toward their future. I have also experienced seeing many athletes and young people miss their purpose, potential, and future because of lack of help and lack of motivation to know they can do it. This is why I was encouraged to write this book and guide, "The Locker Room Experience." It is my goal to help the athlete and coach; and even the parent(s) in areas they need help in, in order to help the athlete get all they need in order to become successful in the sport they are pursuing and in life. This book also focuses on hidden areas hardly talked about in the locker room and at home; which are lacking as a result of a failing team, athlete and coach. As you read, you will receive the truth and the guide you need to help you pursue your personal life, middle school, high school, college and professional career you've been longing for all of your life.

"The Locker Room Experience" is for athlete's and/or coaches who are struggling in and out of the locker room; on and off of the court, field, or track. It is for those athletes and/or coaches in middle school, high School, college, and in professional sports arenas. It is for those athletes and/or coaches who are battling with inferiority, fear, lack of self-confidence, wavering inner struggles such as drugs, alcohol, late night partying and hang-overs before a game, illicit sex, depression, success, overwhelming money issues, debt, popularity, marital issues, relationship issues/battles, bad attitude, temper rages and rampages, having difficulty choosing a moral lifestyle over an immoral life style, heavy weight issues, selfish as an athlete, living with being single and rich, living with being single and successful, difficulty choosing the right mate as a pro athlete, the sudden shock of success, money management problems, choosing the right college or pro team, recruiting issues, struggling with having a heart to win but not a heart for the team as one, struggling with knowing who you are and as an athlete or coach, not confident in your abilities and potential, can't seem to forgive and be healed from the invisible dad or mom and their lack of support, dealing with the guilt and pain of not being there for your child and supporting his or her games, not knowing how to pick the right college, not knowing how to talk to recruiters or scouts, not knowing how to sell yourself as an athlete, not knowing as a parent how to help your child get into college, needing help with coping with coaching and family time, lack of playing time, fear of messing up, fear of growing up, jealous of other teammates success, loving the game but not the salary, loving the position as the coach but discouraged about the salary and the expectations, feeling like a failure when a mistake is made—also known as "dropping the ball", when your "A Game" becomes your "F Game", the frustration of becoming a star, the frustration of keeping the image of being the star in the public eye, lack of support from the missing dad or mom—and how to overcome it, living in a single poverty home and have college potential and even pro potential, when "A's" become "D's and F's", and so on.

I'm sure you can find yourself within either one or more sentences as examples given above whether you are a coach and/or athlete, whether you are a middle school athlete or a pro athlete; and/or whether you are a single parent or a married parent. Those issues are issues that are brought into the locker room and hinder and affect your success, progress, and ability to be the best athlete or coach you can be for every game. Each issue brings conflict and embarrassment. They also have led to detrimental situations such as: suicide, murder, fighting, and more. It is important to release each issue and allow healing to remove the scares, pain, stress, anxiety, and struggles. The Locker Room Experience has come to help restructure the entire team including the coaching staff.

Remember, you are in it to win it and there is no turning back. When the game starts, there is no turning back, there is no time to give up, nor is there time to become fearful—allowing inferiority to set in. Like the old saying says, "Get your head in the game, and lets go win!"

# THE **LOCKER ROOM** *Experience*
## Contents

# THE **LOCKER ROOM** *Experience*
## Before the Game Begins
*Preface*

The most crucial time is right before the game begins. Your thoughts are, "time is ticking", "I gotta' come with my A Game", "I hope my team remembers all the things we practiced on". This is the most important time and tool. It is a time to concentrate on the game with no horsing around. This can be a help or it can be a hindrance if not taken seriously. If your mind is on playing around and having fun rather than having your mind on the game, it can be a hindrance and your game will not be effective. **Concentration and focus is the key.** You have to imagine seeing yourself at the end of the game as a winner and not as whatever, it's just a game, or your game will be just a game with no effort or determination to win. You better believe your opponent is thinking on how to beat you and not just getting through the game. The role of the athlete and the coach plays an equal role. The athlete needs the coach just as the coach needs the athlete to participate and potentially to win. There are no big "I's" or little "Me's". **You both are as ONE.** Neither of you are no more important than the other. You both are important and are a vital asset of the team.

The locker room should be silent right before the game begins. You should be able to hear a pin drop. Everyone including the coach should have already gone over the highlights of the game of the opponent, the do's and the don'ts, and then everybody should be concentrating on the what, the whens, and the how's. Every play you have ever learned and practiced on in practice should be filling up your thoughts and imagination. The game is in your hands. Your career is in your hands. Your future in that particular sport is in how you perform. It's not the game you play, it's how you play game.

After the period of silence is up, it is time to huddle up and get loud and pumped up. It is time to get your adrenalin flowing! It is time to gain strength from your teammates and give them strength as well! It is time to motivate your teammates with yells of encouragement and cheer like, "We can do this!", "this game is ours!", "you can do it!", "I believe in you!" And so on. Your chant should be loud chants of motivation, determination, and with the will to win attitude and not to lose.

"The Locker Room Experience" is for the athlete and coach who are struggling, and do not mind being honest and real about not having the Six Experiences discussed in this book, as well as in their team rules and procedures. Each team should have team rules and procedures. These team rules and procedures clearly state and define what is expected of each athlete and the team as a whole. You may be a coach that is guilty of not pushing the extra mile to take your team beyond the average. You may say, "when we get to the opponent's school or stadium, just go out on the court, field, or track and wait until they start, and then do your thing". Or, "just get out there, it don't matter if you win, it's only a sport, who cares?" If these words fit you, it is time to do a self-evaluation check. I want you to know that it is way more than the nonchalant attitude you are portraying of just going to be a chaperone; it is being a leader, a mentor, a motivator, an example, and a coach who pushes to win and not settle on losing. There are boundaries within this, you can be all of these things but yet not a sore loser. I will discuss this more in the book. Are you ready to get started? Good, let's go!

# The LOCKER ROOM

## ROOM

### *Experience*

For the Struggling Athlete & Coach,
& Tips on How to Get Recruited in Sports.

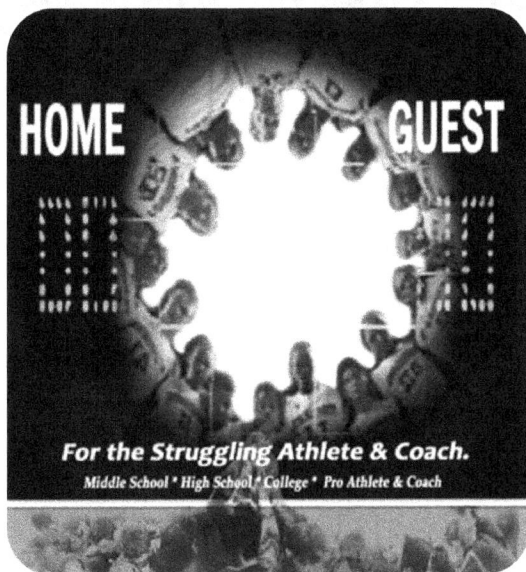

**HOME**     **GUEST**

**For the Struggling Athlete & Coach.**
Middle School * High School * College * Pro Athlete & Coach

# THE **LOCKER ROOM** *Experience*
## *Books by Stephanie*

1. When Ramona Got Her Groove Back from God

2. My Song of Solomon

3. My Song of Solomon *Prayer Journal*

4. Position Your Faith for Great Success

5. Position Your Faith for Great Success *Workbook*

6. The Purpose Chaser: *For Children Ages 5 to 12*

7. God Loves *Thugs* Too!

8. The Locker Room Experience: *For the Struggling Athlete & Coach, & Tips on How to Get Recruited in Sports*

9. Church Hurt: *How to Heal & Overcome It*

I'm reminded of my coaching days of meeting with my coaching staff to go over plays and new ideas to improve the team's strategy to win games. I also remember the sacrifice of making sure the team had all the initials they needed in order to do their best—water, fruit, coolers, sports drinks, providing extra time to go over plays (from the team budget/fundraisers); and making sure they understood what was expected of them.

Every game was approached as a **new season**. Something that had never come before but had potential to be the greatest moment of our lives as a team, and as a coaching staff. It was our time to shine and show off all of the skills and techniques we worked on that previous week. It was show time! In considering a **new season** is not considering sharing a time with someone else; it is a time for us to shine alone. It is to reap a reward of all the hard work and planning we put into preparing for the game **(our season)**.

Your **New Season** is not a time to look back on failed seasons—games that were failed due to lack of participation, conflicts within the coaching staff, laziness to get it over with, and just the plain ol' complacent attitude of just getting through another season. It is a time to look for new talent and push them to be the best. Find ways to bring them out and get them to the purpose and future they were sent on your team to fulfill. **No player/athlete** is on your team by mistake. They are there for a positive reason—never negative, no matter what it look(ed) like. **No coach** is sent to coach a team by mistake. They are there for a positive reason—never negative, no matter what it look(ed) like. **No staff** is on your team by mistake. They are there for a positive reason—never negative, no matter what it look(ed) like. You must look beyond the physical, outer appearance and trust the potential. The potential will only get better when the coach brings that out. You may ask, "How in the world do I do that?" I will answer, "by encouragement, love, and motivating them every step of the way," constantly telling them they are getting better and that you are with them; and you believe in them as their coach/mentor/leader, etc. Miracles come from this type of attitude.

When everything seems to go wrong, it is easy to play the blame game. It is easy to blame others, but the first one to blame should be you. You should always look back on what you have done wrong in order to correct your mistake(s); and seek to better the team. This can be done by workshops, seminars, add more tournaments, schedule team meetings (or more of them) and get the team involved by allowing them to share in an open panel setting; and encourage them to respect each other's opinion while doing so. Remember, encourage the team that whatever is shared in the locker room, stays in the locker room.

*Experience #1*

HOME     GUEST

For the Struggling Athlete & Coach.
Middle School · High School · College · Pro Athlete & Coach

## PART 1
### *Life Is About Rebounds*

**L**IFE IS ABOUT REBOUNDS. When you make a mistake, rebound off that mistake by never taking the same shot or mistake again; and shoot a new shot that will not be blocked or air balled. It is about correcting what either went wrong or is wrong. If you make a terrible shot at attempting to make a basket (or in any sport), fix the shot, don't change your entire game or the sport; or your coaching game plan, just shoot from a different spot or tweak or change the play in the play book. It is not always about changing your entire coaching staff or trading players, or sitting a player down for a mistake made, it is about tweaking or changing the little fox (small mistake) so that it will stop destroying the entire vine—team/play/coaching staff, etc. I have made mistakes in my coaching career at trying to change my entire coaching ability when losing games, when I only needed to change a small part of a play that ultimately changed the entire game around from a loss, to a win. This is the same way our lives are. They are, if you fall, don't give up, fix what is wrong, get back up and try again. It is about not settling for less just because you made or make a mistake. It is about not changing the entire play, picture (entire situation), family, relationship (husband, wife, girlfriend, boyfriend, friend), or job, but tweaking the small foxes that are destroying the entire vine. Meaning, the small things that are destroying your coaching ability, the team, yourself as an athlete or coach, family, relationship, your grades—ability to make "A's", and so forth.

*No one is exempt from life's challenges. They come in all sorts of sizes, colors, weights, people, situations, places, etc. The way to win in this area is to rebound off what the challenge is presented before you, and seek to tweak them until the problem is corrected.*

No one is exempt from life's challenges. They come in all sorts of sizes, colors, weights, people, situations, places, etc. The way to win in this area is to rebound off what the challenge is presented before you, and seek to tweak them until the problem is corrected.

Here are <u>four principles</u> that will help you in your time of challenges as you struggle with the rebound of life and/or within your sport as an athlete and/or coach:

1. **Do Not Look to Rebound, Look to Win.** It is impossible to focus on rebounding a missed shot when your initial goal should be to make the shot in the first place. Confusion comes when you are confused and lack confidence in

yourself as an athlete or person. You must increase your faith (confidence, trust, reliance, belief) and not settle with conquering that one challenge of first thinking "I must rebound", and changing your mindset to, "I must make the shot to win". "I must conquer not just one challenge that comes my way, I must conquer all challenges that come my way to win in every situation; or battle I may face within that sport or in life. You must look ahead to conquer every challenge that comes your way. The key is, be patient before reacting, listen to the other person, state your claim in a calm way (make your point with all humbleness), set a goal to be a peacemaker in the matter and avoid conflict.

2. **Trust Yourself. Believe in Yourself. Stay Focus. Share.** It is important to guard these areas to stay on top of your game, to help focus on what type of shot you are taking, and to sink the shot with a winning bucket. Rebounding is nowhere in the picture when these points are practiced on a daily basis.

Trust and believe in yourself by knowing that you have worked hard, and have practiced and know the plays and have the ability to do anything you set your mind too.

Stay focus when those challenges come, because they will come. Do not listen to the voice that tells you, you can't do it or you can't win or you will never make it. Focus on what you know to be true and believe. Focus on your inner Spirit that tells you you can and you are doing the right thing and a great job. If this is you, I say keep doing what you are doing.

Sharing is not always something that should be private. There are times when you will need to open up and share in order to release that which is troubling you. It is not good to hold everything inside because sooner or later, it will all come out and it may not be a good sight for those around you. I will share a true story. There

> *"Team Talks" are important to have. You have to realize that you are not just teammates, you are a family.*

was a young lady on my team that was going through a really tough time at home. The team and I noticed something was not right because of her negative attitude, isolation, sudden missed practices; and the fact that that was not her character at first. It took a toll on the entire team. She would not open up and share but instead tried to fight through it on her own. Well, her way did not work. Eventually she exploded on everybody. She could not remember the plays. Would not listen to my coaching instructions and became very rebellious. It came to a point when she had to talk or I was going to have to take action. Before action was taken, I thought of a way that would help not to point her out as the individual targeted problem, but to allow everyone to open up and share altogether. Before that could happen, she ended up personally writing me a letter telling me what was wrong, and from there the thought of that good idea to have everybody on the team open up and share what was on their mind became a reality; and encouraged them to know that what we talked about was in confidential. They did. I received a huge response and it even worked with the

*LEARNING IS LISTENING.*

coaching staff. I realize from that day forward that sometimes people/athletes/coaches/teachers/parents are crying on the inside to open up about what's wrong on the inside, but they just don't know how. Writing out your feelings is a great step to expressing the way you feel until they become easy to verbally open up and talk about. I call them, **"Team Talks"**. **"Team Talks"** are important to have. You have to realize that you are not just teammates, you are a family. Team Talks are confidential, between the coach and the team. After this exercise and experience, it drew the entire team closer together and made coaching easier; and it also motivated each player on the team to do their best through love, loyalty, understanding and unity. And it helped the player to not quit, commit suicide, or something even more detrimental had this method not been considered. And also, for the rest of the team, it helped eliminate the robbery of suicide rates, pregnancy, fighting, jail time, and murders.

3. **Listen.** Listening is an important factor to gaining knowledge. When you listen, you can hear important information and instructions that is needed to hear, other than when you are running your mouth at the same time as the coach and miss it. As an athlete it is important to listen to your leader (coach, teacher, parent(s), mentor, etc.). You cannot learn while talking while your coach is talking. **LEARNING IS LISTENING.** There is no way around it.

If you were picked to lead, this applies more to you. If you are the captain of the team, this applies more to you. Captains and leaders do not know everything. In fact, everybody has someone they have to listen too. You are held accountable to listen. Make sense? Good, I knew you would agree. Coaches also have to listen. You don't know everything. There are times when the team can teach or help you and still know that you are their coach. For example, there was a time I was coaching my team in a basketball game. We were winning with the same play I instructed the team to run. However, as the game continued on, the opponent team adapted to the play and began to capitalize off of it by making us turn over the ball with a score in their favor. Although I knew how to coach, I became cold and went blank. One of the team members said while we huddled up during a timeout that I called, "coach won't you go with the other play we worked on in practice, I know that will work." If I was a proud coach, I would have told her to be quiet and to let me coach my team. But I didn't. Actually, she helped me snapped out of the dry moment I was having. I quickly agreed and instructed everybody to run the play and was glad I did because it worked, and brought the team back up to the lead and won the game. Had I allowed pride and arrogance to get in the

> *Pride and arrogance will get you nowhere as a coach.*

way; we would have for sure lost the game. The learning experience in that was, **coaches do not know everything**. You can learn by listening, no matter who gives it. Pride and arrogance will get you nowhere as a coach. In fact, you are more respected when you can listen to your team. My team respected that part about me as their coach because I listened to how they felt, took their feelings in consideration, and as a result it made my coaching easier.

4.  **Work on It.** Work on your weaknesses. I was always taught as an athlete that <u>practice makes perfect</u>. The way you practice is that way you are going to play or perform in the game. If you goof off and play around in practice,

that is how you will perform in the game, if you get in. If you do not listen to instructions in practice, you will be confused in the game. Then you will have to experience bench time. Nobody wants bench time. Do not make excuses, work hard on those areas of weakness in practice and even on your own time, and they will become your strengths in the game. Me as an athlete, I believed that I could not be beat. I was a competitor. I believed that I could do anything but fail. My mind was focused on the prize of winning. I worked hard by practicing extra on my own while at home by going to practice early before everybody got there. I worked hard during practice, and there were times I even stayed afterwards working on those areas of weakness so that I could improve them and make them my strengths. I encourage you to do the same. It worked for me and I excelled as an athlete and as a person. I also did the same in my studies. Whenever I had a low grade, I asked the teacher if there were extra credit work I could do, I went to tutoring when it was offered, and I made sure that I asked questions during class when I was confused. I encourage you again to do the same. It worked for me and I excelled by making honor roll and graduating in the top half of my class, and on to receiving a Bachelor and Master's Degree in college.

## *No Touchdown Is the Same*

**N**O **TOUCHDOWN IS THE SAME.** Life challenges may come, but the way you handle them should never be the same way. You should take each challenge as they come and conquer its challenges by having a game plan to maneuver your way through that particular life's challenge; and come out on top with a new attitude, mind, and determination for the next touchdown or challenge. For example, you may be a high school or college athlete/student and are used to making A's on your test and/or in other classes. Suddenly you have reached a dry moment and are not able to make A's, and now C's are kicking in and the thought of a great GPA is impossible; and studying the same way will not cut it as far as making A's again. You cannot do the same thing you were doing while in those other classes— which are why your grades went down in the first place, you will have to handle each class a different way. If you studied by yourself with no help, now you will need to get others that are making A's on the tests and/or in other classes, and ask to set up a study time with them. You may also take out more time to study than you are giving yourself. Tutoring is not bad. It can help to perfect what is already ready to be perfected.

Here's one for the coach that is trying to make a touchdown the same way but is having bad luck. Again, you cannot handle that challenge the same way. Most times minor changes are only needed. Changing the entire play, picture or situation is not always necessary. If your play book is set up to hand the ball off to the player/running back to go to the left

> It is TEAM-work that wins games, not ME-work. There is no SELF in TEAM.

and the opponent team is stopping that part of the play, you do not need to change or take out the entire play. All you need to do is tweak the same play by setting up the same player/running back to start going to the left but quickly turn with a reverse, or fake a hand off to him and pass the ball instead. Sometimes the small changes win ball games.

In the professional sports arena, not every athlete is on every night. You have to learn to share the ball, especially when there is more than one star on the team. It should be your livelihood. They are your family. You are with them majority of your time and life. **TEAM-work wins games, not ME-work. There is no SELF in TEAM.** You should never be selfish as a team player or as a coach. **A WIN NEVER EVOLVES AROUND ONE TEAM PLAYER; IT ALWAYS EVOLVES AROUND THE ENTIRE TEAM, HEAD COACH, AND COACHING STAFF.** Therefore, you cannot get upset and want to be traded or quit because you did not get the ball, or because they did not pick you for the winning point at the last minute due to the competition for that night. It is what's best at that moment for the entire TEAM. It is about making sacrifices for yourself and for your teammates that matters. It is not about you. It is about the entire team that matters. There is not an "I" in "TEAM", please remember that, especially in your most heated moment or tantrum. It is easy to get selfish, especially when you are who the team/plays are centered around. One thing you must remember if this is the case for you, it is the entire team who wins. There is no possible way that you can pass the ball to yourself and run and make a touchdown or make a point on your own, someone else must pass you the ball and you must catch it to complete the pass and make the touchdown or get the point. It is the same with life; you cannot live this life alone, especially if you are a pro athlete or a pro coach or staff. You will need one another. You will need to love, depend, and appreciate one another. You will need a spiritual grounding—a support group, teammates, church, family, friends, mentor and a strong relationship if you so choose. I am not saying that you cannot make it if you do not have anyone, what I am saying is that it will be very challenging for you at most times.

*There is not an "I" in "TEAM".*

There is nothing wrong with new game plans to make new touchdowns on the court, field, track, and life. Use whatever works for you. No one can tell you that your plan is useless when it is working for you. For example, whatever game plan works to keep your marriage together, work that plan and do not worry about what people think or say. If it works for you and your spouse or significant other, then do it and do it with all you have. This also goes for the athlete on the playing field. What works for you, as long as you're listening to the coach and running the plays like they should be ran, then continue doing you.

# Experience #3

HOME    GUEST

For the Struggling Athlete & Coach.
Middle School • High School • College • Pro Athlete & Coach

## Make Your Volley Count

**M**AKE YOUR VOLLEY COUNT. Women pack a powerful punch when it comes to athletics. Although they are considered to be the weaker vessels, they still are more than meets the eye when it comes to being a competitor. I, as a woman athlete know how it feels when you compete against men and those men who have this "I ain't gon' let no girl beat me" attitude. It's funny because as a young girl I had to quickly show them that they were wrong. Of course I put a beaten on em' (smile). Had some of them crying

*Make your volley count—everyday relationships should volley each other with the goal of not dropping the ball in mind.*

and apologizing for the unkind remark given. I still laugh about those memories. I have learned that it is not about gender that wins games, it is about being a competitor and a team player that wins games. Whatever volley you make, make it count. Whatever decision you make at that moment, make it count like it's your last decision on earth. Never take a game play lightly. Each play is important.

Make your volley count—everyday relationships should volley each other with the goal of not dropping the ball in mind. For example, as a team player while playing the game of volleyball hits the ball in the air one time as they pass the ball to the other teammate, notice the ball never drops on the ground? If it does, the team will lose that point or possession; which will give the opponent team a chance to win the game. This is why you must make your volley count every time it is within you to make a difference. You should make a difference with a positive attitude and winning spirit; and tell yourself, **"I will not drop the ball no matter what"**. As the ball is in your possession, make your pass count as perfect as you can to your teammates, relationships, friendships, marriage, co-workers, church, etc. so that you all can win on a daily basis.

# *Experience #4*

HOME     GUEST

For the Struggling Athlete & Coach.
Middle School • High School • College • Pro Athlete & Coach

## *Run Your Race with Endurance and Determination to Win:* **Just Do You**

**R**UN YOUR RACE WITH ENDURANCE AND DETERMINATION TO WIN: JUST DO YOU. Never start a race to lose, have a goal to come in second, or just to finish the race. This is not the faith and endurance you should have as an athlete or as a person. Everyone is counting on you to win, not just to finish the race. Although finishing is good, but it takes your faith a step higher to be better than the best by thinking on the lines of, "I'm going to win", and do it. You have already finished the race. You have done it many times in practice. Now as it counts for the actual race of life you are in, make it count with a win. Your family, coach, teacher, pastor, minister leader, mentor, parent(s), guardian, whichever you choose to acknowledge has high hopes and expectations for you. **Only the strong survives. You must be**

> *Although finishing the race is good, but it takes your faith a step higher to be better than the best by thinking on the lines of "I'm going to win" and do it.*

**strong and not give up,** even when life gets unbearable and hard to handle, and it seems as if no one understands; and suicide, joining a gang, stealing, illicit sex, pornography, teen pregnancy, sexual and/or relational abuse or even murder seems to be the better way, **don't do it.** Go talk to someone who can help you. Find a good close friend, or family member, parent(s), coach, counselor, pastor, youth pastor, teacher, or mentor. You will be glad you did. Believe it or not, you do have someone who loves you and wants the best for you. It may not look like it right now, but if you stop, relax, and think about it, you do have someone you can go talk to that will listen to you and help you. Most times all you need is for someone to listen to you. You just need to vent by getting it all out. **Release** is important for you as an athlete. **Release** is important for you as a coach or coaching staff. School athletics, school districts, and professional leagues have this horrible secret that needs to come out among students, athletes and coaches in order to stop this terrible cycle of suicide, murder suicide (individual and in relationships), abuse, alcoholism, drugs, bullying, and jail time.

The key to winning the race comes with persistence. You must pace yourself in order to be persistent to stay persistent. If rushing is your biggest setback, slow down and pace yourself and take your time; your result will be more rewarding than if you rush and lose all you have or the race or the game. Go back to square one, where you came from and start over, concentrate and do it right but this time take it slow.

A race is not always won by who can run the fasted or who can hit the most buckets in a basketball game, or who can maneuver their way through the biggest lines men to make a touchdown, it is by the one who can pace themselves and be persistent until the end. I have found this to be true when I ran track. I remember running against an opponent who was picked to win over me because they were faster. Before the race began, the thoughts of, "I am not going to win this race, she is way faster than me" ran through my mind. But as we all got down on our starting blocks ready to start the race, my mind went straight to, "just run your race, pace yourself, and be persistent and you will win". As the gun sounded, of course she shot out of the blocks first and appeared as if she had the race wrapped up with a win; and no one would be able to catch her. But then, suddenly she lost wind and began to slow down as I had paced myself from the beginning, began to increase my speed and started gaining on her as the finish line approached near in the distance. The more I increased my speed from the pace that I had set from the beginning; the picked winner became the loser. I won the race and the crowd went crazy. They were cheering with surprise, but with joy and happiness for me and for the team. So, this is why I say it is important to not get intimidated or become inferior by what the opponent looks like, **"JUST DO YOU"**. Just compete at the pace you have practiced and have set for yourself and be persistent in it. No one knows you better than you. All you have to

*"JUST DO YOU"*

do is trust yourself. I trusted myself and did not look at my opponent. Had I looked at her, I would have lost the race in the very beginning when she shot out of the blocks and seemed as if she was going to win. I trust myself, I trust God, and I depend on His power and strength to help me. It is your quickness and abilities and determination to win and not give up—**NO MATTER WHAT IT LOOKS LIKE**. It worked for me as I never lost a race in track and field in all my years in middle school. This brings me to the next chapter, "Determination to Win".

# *Experience #5*

## *Determination to Win: Will to Win*

**D**ETERMINATION TO WIN: Will to Win. Giving the example of running the race with persistence in order to win the race in the last chapter brings me to another example. I was a young lady who competed in many different sports. I love sports of all kinds. I come from a family of sports. I have competed on the elementary, middle school, AAU, TAC, high school, and on the college level. They all had their share of competition and great expectation. Each level raised its level of expectancy and work ethic. I could not keep the same work ethic in high school as I did in middle school. I had to grow up and change my mindset and determination to the level of winning on a greater, faster, and stronger level. No matter how I felt on a particular day, I could not back down and lower my standards to lose and not win. **I had to have a <u>will to win</u>.** I had to remain <u>persistent</u>, balance my time, take my priorities serious (at home and at

> *No matter how I felt on a particular day, I could not back down and lower my standards to lose and not win... I had to be persistent... bring my "A Game" every game...*

school), work hard during every practice, learn and know all the plays, bring my "A Game" every game, keep a positive and obedient attitude in check for a good conduct every six weeks, make honor roll every six weeks, set goals to raise my GPA, put my life as an athlete in perspective in the locker room as well as out of the locker room; and know there was a balance. It worked. I graduated from high school and went on to graduate from college with a college degree and on to Graduate school, graduating with a master's degree. Not only did I get degrees, but I also started my own successful businesses, founded my own non-profit center, and ministry. You can do it too.

*I encourage you to have a **WILL TO WIN**.*

Anger plays a big part against the **determination to win**. Failure to fix the area of anger in your life will bring you to a place of being alone. No one wants to be around a person who is always angry, or is quick to get a bad attitude over everything. Anger also stirs up the energy of stress. It is the biggest stress builder ever. Anger will lead you to a quick heart attack or even to a stroke, or even possibly death. You can avoid this detrimental accident by staying calm in your most heated times, calming down when anger shows its face, talking out your problems, releasing whatever is troubling you and not holding on to those things that bother you (people—what they say, bullies, hurt, unforgiveness, no support, lack of love, lack of understanding, being misunderstood, the feeling of everything you do is wrong, the not good enough syndrome, nagging parents, nagging wife or husband, sister, brother, etc.). This is the will to win when you get to a place where you do not allow those things to bother you or get you down. If you are guilty of these examples, they can play a big part in the success of your game. They can bring your game down as an athlete or coach. **I ENCOURAGE YOU TO HAVE A WILL TO WIN.**

Good eating habits play a big part in the success and successful performance of the athlete and coaching staff. You must take care of your body and watch what you put in it. If you eat junk, you'll feel and look like junk on the playing field or court. Eat a wholesome meal everyday—morning, noon, and night. Make sure you eat vegetables and less starch. Drink plenty of water and less to no juice or soda. A good weight plan and diet is great to follow while you are active in your sporting season, and every day of your life. Just as you should have a determination to win, you must also have that same determination to work-out on a consistent and daily basis; and a determination to eat right with a wholesome diet.

**HERE IS A SAMPLE DAILY DIET CHART TO HELP YOU:**

| | MORNING | NOON | NIGHT |
|---|---|---|---|
| **MONDAY** <br> *(5 Bottles of water per day.)* | peanut butter toast 1 egg, or cereal & milk, Glass/bottle of water | Sandwich with chips w/no salt, glass of water | full meal with vegetables, juice with no sugar, Glass/bottle of water |
| **TUESDAY** | Repeat Monday's plan | | |
| **WEDNESDAY** | Repeat Tuesday's Plan | | |
| **THURSDAY** | Repeat Wednesday's Plan | | |
| **FRIDAY** | Repeat Thursday's Plan | | |
| **SATURDAY** | Repeat Friday's Plan | | |
| **SUNDAY** | Repeat Saturday's Plan | | |

Coaches, I encourage you to encourage your team to eat a wholesome meal everyday. It is also good for you as well. You are not exempt from this. You have to set an example for your team. You may not realize it, but your example goes a long way. You are inspiring in ways you do not know. You are being watched in ways you do not know. This is why it is important to practice what you preach. I realize that you are not perfect and there is no perfect coach, but you do the best that you can and up-hold the accountability of the coach you signed up and were hired to be. You are not just a coach; you are a leader that has the opportunity to change a life that will never be the same. I can recall a few that helped me along the way. There wasn't many, in fact, I can count them on one hand and still have fingers left. But, the faithful few that helped me, I will always remember. I inspire and mentor children, youth, young adults, adults, athletes, and some coaches to be the best they can be at all times.

Do not allow your frustration of not having the ultimate dream team you desired to stop you from being an effective, dynamic leader that you can be. You never know, through your faithfulness, sacrifice, hardworking leadership you can get the dream team that you desire. Sometimes winners may not jump right out at you, you have to perfect them. You may have to bring them out of your team. But, when you take the time to do that, you will be glad you did. A little more than just the regular practice and go home will have to do if you want that dream team you desire and winners. You will have to put in extra time, make sure each athlete is taken care of—their stats are up-dated, have every game videotaped (do fundraisers to buy a video recorder, get the managers to video tape every game for you and the team, take a practice one day a week to review your videos of where to perfect your team and their game), inspiring them to go to college and/or do better as a pro athlete, look at film with the team and with the coaching staff (before you watch with the team), do workshops and go to trainings, go on fieldtrips to colleges or other schools and get pointers and help, network and collaborate with other teams doing the same as you, watch other teams that are already dream teams—teams that are undefeated, lift weights with your team and show them the right way to lift, go on a diet with them (maybe bring water and fruit and put it in coolers for the team to eat for each game especially away games) encourage them to stay away from sodas and junk food, teach them how to lead by example (attitude, leadership, accountability), be on time, remain after practice with those who want to stay and/or stay and work with those to help make them better. You can do it. I believe in you as a coach. I understand how you feel. I am with you. But, one thing I practiced that was so effective for me was that I loved and appreciated each one of my athletes just the way they were. I saw the best in them. I did not see them where they were in the slow state some of them were in, I saw them where the best of them were going. This helped me to push them and make them strong. I did not down them and tell them they were nobody's or curse at them, or curse them out.

Even when at times I may have doubted on the inside, I never let them know it. I believed with them. Always remembered they will remember everything you say and tell them. So always, watch what you say. Do the best you can. This is how I was able to have an undefeated season. This is how many of my athletes was encouraged to pursue scholarships and college education; along with hopes of being a pro athlete one day. You must be the leader you were sent to that school or pro organization to be and better. There will be challenging moments. Times when you want to quit. But that is the time when you have to get your second wind and encourage yourself. Video tape your games and when you get discouraged, go back to your best winning game and that winning game your team had that season; and feast off that until it brings your faith back to believe again. This is your locker room experience every time you set foot on the campus and thereafter you will follow and remember this.

# Experience #6

HOME　　GUEST

For the Struggling Athlete & Coach.
Middle School • High School • College • Pro Athlete & Coach

## Inside & Outside of the
## Locker Room Matters

INSIDE & OUTSIDE OF THE LOCKER ROOM MATTERS. It is important to understand your other life outside of the locker room is just as important as your locker room experience. Your personal and private life whether with your spouse, family, parents, siblings, friends, and/or relationships is just as important as preparing for the game. Your game will not be effective if your life outside of the locker room is not effective. It takes work in both areas. In fact, your life outside of the locker room takes first prestige and is more important simply because if this area is not on point, it will affect your entire game. Do you agree? Good. Let me give you an example, you may have just gotten word from your teacher that you must pass your test or final exam in order to continue playing your sport, you currently have a failing grade and this is a crucial time in your life. You don't know what to do, you don't quite understand the material, you've done all you can to understand, and the big game is tonight, what do you do? What do you feel? Who do you turn too? Where do you go? Who do you have to turn too and listen? Who will understand? Embarrassment is weighing at you because you don't want to look dumb, or be the failing leader on the team, or hear any smart remarks, or even let your team and coach down. Stress is pounding at your heart so that you have heart palpitations and headaches. Your coach and teammates are depending on you to perform—to come with the big hits, the big touchdowns, the big spikes to put away the game, the winning shot, to win your running race, and pumped up words of encouragement. All the pressure is on you. Just as you may be experiencing the pressure from having to pass the test, you may be experiencing something much deeper—a failing marriage or relationship, contemplation of suicide, hidden abuse, pressure to meet your parent's standards or your popular parents standards, the pressure and fear of failure, your

*The heart of a champion—to keep going even when the going gets tough.*

parent's that is never happy with anything you do, a nagging illness, jealous teammates, an unfair coaches decision, or an injury that may have ended your career. This is the secret life of the athlete that is never told or ever comes out until it's too late. I am an athlete of over thirty years and a coach and rehabilitation coach of over twenty years. I have experienced and have seen many challenges within the athlete throughout these years in all areas of my life. I understand the pressure to perform in and outside of the locker room—hardship, passion of wanting to win no matter the cost; and the heart of a champion—to keep going even when the going gets tough. Many would ask, "how do I get through the challenges I'm facing and still be the excelling athlete and/or coach"? My only method for you is to turn to the Lord for help (Romans 10:9). You may say, "but I don't know", or "that seems way too religious". My answer to you would be that there is no certain way to turn but to turn with your whole heart. What I mean by this is, when you look to God for help, you must mean every word that you are praying to Him. He is fair and He is a Friend. God is a listener. He will hear every word that you are saying without cutting you off. God meets you as the believer where you are. A believer is someone who believes in God. Do you believe in God? If you said yes, you are a believer. Just as you believe in the sport that you are playing, you must believe that God will help you on and off the court or field, in and out of the locker room.

Problems do not stop because you are a leader. They do not stop because you are the team captain. They do not stop because you get a lot of playing time. They do not stop because you ride the bench and get no playing time. They do not stop because you are the coach and have an undefeated season. They do not stop because your coaching staff has lost faith in you because of the losing season you have had as a head coach. They do not stop because you are a rookie coach or player, playing or coaching for the first time in a game of your life to either stay on the team or to continue coaching without getting fired. Life is what it is. This is why you must maintain a sense of balance, honesty/trust, listening, and belief. I want to briefly talk about these four things: Balance, honesty/trust, listening, and belief.

**BALANCE.** Balance is the key to having a successful career as an athlete or coach in and out of the locker room. Family time is important outside of the locker room. Spouse time is important outside of the locker room. You two may have different demanding lives that spending quality time may difficult. But I will tell you that if you want that marriage or have peace within your family, making time is a must. You cannot have a successful relationship if you do not know when to turn on and turn off the locker room, buddies, and meeting with the coaching staff on a daily basis. You may travel a lot and time to call or flying back home to see your family or spouse is out of the question. I will tell you a call is worth a million dollars, especially when children and youth are involved. You may be a youth in high school or a male or female in college, this works the same for all who are a part of the locker room experience. Balance is discipline. You must discipline yourself everyday by making notes, purchasing a planner and make a time line of the things you need to do daily and work hard just has you do on the court or field to meet those

*You cannot have a successful relationship if you do not know when to turn on and turn off the locker room, buddies, and meeting with the coaching staff on a daily basis.*

goals. Study for test ahead of time, just as you prepare for your game to bring an "A Game", I always tell my athletes and the youth I coach and mentor, you must bring your "A Game" in studying for tests and making it a priority to make good grades beyond just passing. Your GPA (Grade Point Average) is just as important as the touchdown you long to make or sacking the quarterback in football, or the powerful dunk or winning shot you long to make in basketball, or the hard point clenching spike you dream of hitting in volleyball, or the first place in track & field or cross country, and so on. Remember to balance each day with a prayer before you start your day, grab your planner before you leave—do your best to fulfill everything goal on that planner for that day whether it be:

1. Turning in homework on time,
2. studying for tests,
3. signing up for the SAT and/or ACT,
4. learning plays for the team you're on,
5. making sure you as a coach are making new plays, watching film, knowing your craft, enjoying family time just as you do your team,
6. and ending your day with a conscious decision to live in peace, and prayer realizing we can never do anything on our own. It takes a Higher Power Who is God Himself to keep us from attacks, attacking others, suicide, giving up, failure in yourself and your teammates, pressure of a

heart attack because you just can't take the pressure, and so on [Philippians 4:6].

**HONESTY/TRUST.** Honesty/trust goes a long way in the locker room experience. You must be honest with yourself, your coach, and teammates when there is something wrong with you before a detrimental situation happens. You must tell the one that can be trusted. Not all coaches or teammates can be trusted, but there should be someone you can trust to open up and talk to before things get out of hand, or even someone lose their life. You may even turn to a person who may not be in the locker room with you. They may be your parent(s), very trusted friend, counselor, mentor, pastor, youth pastor, or whomever, you must find that trusted person to be honest with and vent to. This helps with releasing the pressure of the locker room experience. You may be in college and this is your freshman year and things are all new—plays are new, meeting a lot of women or men and the overwhelming of popularity that comes with it, the grasping of studying and taking multiple test in one day, the popular fraternity and sorority parties that you can't stay away from, the dorm life of doing whatever you want to do, women running up to you, or men hunting you down for attention and a number. You may even be a pro athlete or pro coach or staff. It is important to find a person, peer group, counselor, team counselor, pastor, mentor to open up too constantly to release the pressure of the popularity, important business matters, making the right decisions on endorsements, meeting new friends, a relationship with a woman or man, finding the right person to settle down with, getting the spiritual knowledge and prayer that is needed on a daily basis. All of these things are important and plays a big part in your success, performance, and ability to maintain a successful career on and off the court or field or in or out of the locker room, and the ability to stay grounded on what you believe and cancel out all negative relationships, friendships, groupies, clicks, or even peer pressure from meeting the needs and wants from those who mean you no good.

**LISTENING.** One of the greatest highlights to any successful athlete is a listening athlete. You must listen to your coach and teammates. You may not always agree, but listening will help keep away conflict and added pressure when playing in the game with them. No one has time to deal with conflict or negative vibes from another player or coach or between a coach and the coaching staff. Listening allows both parties to hear what they have to say and respect how they feel. It is okay to agree to disagree. You are not going to agree with everything everybody says because we are all different and we all have our own opinions, but when you listen and respect that person, learn to move on, your relationship as teammates, or coaching staff will be strengthened and will go far—even as far to winning games and championships.

**BELIEF.** What you stand for and what you believe makes who you are. Let me say this again, what you stand for and what you believe makes who you are. This is why it is important to make sure you are believing in positive things and being a positive role model. For example, giving high fives in a game to your teammates who perform excellent, encourage those who miss a shot or pass or winning point, or even those who may not get a chance to play that particular game, or encouraging your teammates even when you're having a bad game or don't get in the game at all. You must believe in your teammates and coaching staff. Believing in them will boost them and motivate them to be better athletes, teammates, coaches, boys, girls, men, and/or women in society.

## PART II
### *Bad Choices Come With a Price*

> *Things that constitute a bad locker room experience: bad choices in relationships, team conflicts, lack of confidence and self-control in yourself and in each other, jealousy of success and popularity, lack of love for yourself and teammates; and love for the game:*

**B**AD CHOICES COME WITH A PRICE. There is a price you pay for making bad decisions and choosing who you want in your circle and by your side. Relationships must be chosen carefully and not quickly. You must take your time and do not move too fast. Many times we move too fast and lose what could be a beautiful, long lasting relationship if you had of slowed down and let the time of getting to know one another better, bring you two closer together. Being too picky pays a big part in choosing bad relationships. I'll never understand why people draw close to those who are mean and controlling rather than drawing close to those who are nice, respectful and will do anything for them. This thought will always cross my mind as long as I live. I figure in my experience in watching relationships in and out of the locker room, and talking to different athletes as an athlete and as a coach, that it is the longing for a challenge that draws them. Most people do not want somebody who will tell them yes all the time, they want somebody who will tell them no most of the time and challenge their every way and conversation. This is not a good relationship and it only eventually leads to a dead end. Most always either live an argumentative lifestyle everyday, or they eventually split up with a nasty commotion or even in a deadly way. It is not wrong to take your time and be single until your choice is right. You will know it deep down on the inside when it is right. It will not be based on your emotions, feelings, or lust of the body and eyes; it will be based on the spiritual knowing deep down on the inside that only God can give. I hope you believe this. You may ask, "what does making bad choices in relationships have to do with the locker room experience?" I will answer by saying, "they have everything to do with the locker room experience. When you've just had a bad argument or experience within a opposite sex, friendship, or relationship, it has a great effect on your performance as an athlete and it starts before the locker room; and gets worse the closer you get to your performance."

*Experience* #8

HOME    GUEST

For the Struggling Athlete & Coach.
Middle School • High School/College • Pro Athlete & Coach

## Team Conflicts

**T**EAM CONLFICTS. Team conflicts can give a team a terrible record and season. It can tear a state championship, NBA championship, or Super Bowl winning team a part. It can fire a coach who has the ability to coach the team to winning games. It can either injure or inadvertently kill or purposely kill another athlete. It can bring unnecessary pressure on other teammates who have nothing to do with the conflict. It can cause you to get dropped from the team.

Bad attitudes, pride—the big head and ignorance causes team conflict. An athlete with a bad attitude can never reach the level or purpose they are expected to reach in this life unless they change. A bad attitude will make others believe or see something that may not be who that person really is on the inside. You ever heard of someone saying, "I am being falsely accused or falsely judged because of my bad attitude." Well, with a bad attitude, no one can see the really nice, talented, gifted person, athlete, or coach you really are. All they see is the terrible attitude you display in the locker room, at practice, in games, yelling at everything, cursing out the players or teammates and belittling their efforts. This type of behavior will eventually drop you from the team, get you fired as a coach, start a riot on the team, get you and the team disqualified, delete the respect you deserve, or shun everybody away from you. Make a conscious decision that you are going to strive for excellence with a positive attitude as an athlete, coach, coaching staff, or even as a person.

# Experience #9

HOME | GUEST

For the Struggling Athlete & Coach.
Middle School * High School * College * Pro Athlete & Coach

## Lack of Confidence and Self-Control
## In Yourself and Others

L ACK CONFIDENCE AND SELF-CONTROL IN YOURSELF AND OTHERS. Lacking confidence in yourself and in others constitute a bad locker room experience. When you lack confidence in who God made you to be, lack confidence in your game and the ability to perform, brings a bad experience in the locker room. Whether you know it or not you cannot hide lack of confidence. It can be seen through your teammates and your coach, if you are a coach it can be seen through the fans, your team, and the coaching staff. This can cause you to perform beneath your real ability as an athlete—team player or as a coach that you really are meant to be. No one wants to be recognized beneath who they really are. You want to be recognized, respected, and loved as the athlete and coach of who you really are. Confidence, not pride or arrogance in yourself plays a big part. You may ask, "how do I obtain confidence in myself without getting proud or arrogant?" I will answer, "by having an attitude of thankfulness and humility (humble spirit); and always remembering that at any given moment all the fame, abilities, fortune, accolades can be taken away from you."

Self-Control is another killer among athletes and coaching staff's. Many have brought detrimental and embarrassing experiences on and off the court, field, or locker room. Parents are included in this self-control thing. It is important to maintain self-control with yourself especially when your child may not be performing great like another athlete is, getting accolades, a bad call by the referees, the coach may have made a bad decision that may have cost the game or season, difference among the team, and so on. It is important to maintain self-control. Athletes must have self-control in the same way. The coach and referees are not perfect. They make mistakes and some may need a little help in their area of craft (smile), but you are still required as an athlete, coach/leader, and parent to maintain self-control at all times. It is important to understand that others are watching you. They are watching your decisions, actions, attitude, the things you say. They are watching how you carry yourself, how you carry the team as a coach, what you believe, your ability to praise others other than yourself—even when you have a bad game and theirs are good, and all the attention is on them and not on you; and how you know your game position as an athlete or your coaching position as a coach.

*Experience #10*

HOME · GUEST

For the Struggling Athlete & Coach.
Middle School · High School · College · Pro Athlete & Coach

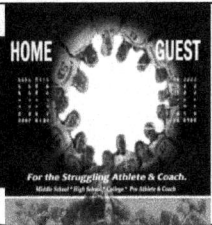

## Jealousy of Other's Success
## and Popularity

J EALOUSY OF OTHER'S SUCCESS AND POPULARITY. It is normal for athletes to become jealous of another athlete or teammate. Some even become jealous of the coaches success and popularity. The problem is, when the jealousy becomes noticeable and out of hand. A person cannot help when thoughts and feelings come upon them, but they do have the power not to receive them. You can rebuke them and choose to have positive thoughts and feelings toward yourself, teammates, your coaches, family, friends and the people around you on a daily basis. If this is not carefully managed or changed, this can bring a bad locker room experience; which has potential of blowing issues out of control and a heated battle of an out of control fight. To remove jealousy is to boost up and encourage your teammates, coaching staff, friends, and people around you as much as possible by telling them that they are doing a great job, or did a great job, or made a great shot, or passed an awesome pass, or hit a great spike, or served an excellent serve, or did a great job on that run, etc. Athletes want to be loved, belonged, and appreciated. They do not want to be belittled about every little thing they did wrong, but what they did right. It is important to remember this. As long as you are rooting your teammates on and pumping them up every chance you get, jealousy should not play any part in your attitude, emotions, or conversation. Coaches are not exempt from jealousy. There are some cases where the coach becomes jealous of an athlete to a point where he or she does not allow them to be interviewed or cheat them on playing time. I have experience this in my years of playing sports. There was a coach who got jealous of the attention I was receiving from the audience and took me out of the game and lost the game because of it. It was so obvious that the coach was out of control, that the audience started yelling at the coach to put me back in the game, although they (he/she) did not obey. I am grateful because it did not affect my future, although it did affect my playing time and attitude; and caused much out of hand confusion—even in the locker room. Not all coaches are fair and some should not be coaching; and some do not want to coach but do it for the money/salary. This is not good for the athletes who are on a team with a coach who does not want to coach. Each one of them is cheated of getting the fullness out of that sport in which they need to help them toward their future. People can tell when a coach does not want to coach. He or she does not do extra to help the athletes or team as a whole. People can also tell when an athlete's heart is not into a particular sport. He or she does not put in the extra dedication and competitiveness needed to win. I encourage every coach that is stuck in a sport without their wanting or a coach who chose a sport just for the money/salary and does not have the heart and passion for the sport or for the team, to quit. You are wasting your time and you are cheating your team of athletes who are trying to pursue a successful career in that particular sport. You should seek to find a sport or profession that you have the passion for so that not only you can benefit, but all of the team of athletes can also.

## Lack of Love for Yourself, Teammates, and For the Game

**L**ACK OF LOVE FOR YOURSELF, TEAMMATES, AND FOR THE GAME. When an athlete lacks love for themselves and their teammates they should leave the sport and find a sport that they will love and have a love for. I will give you an example, I ran track and field all through my child, teen, and by my senior year, I lost the love for the sport and did not want to pursue it further for college. Instead of me pushing and pursuing and accepting college scholarships to colleges, I left it and pursued basketball among many other sports that I also loved. I peeked out in track and field although I still do it to keep my body in shape but not for a career. Had I continued on with that sport and with my heart somewhere else, I would have been a hindrance to myself, the coaching staff, and to the team. This is the same for any athlete and also for any coach. I'm sure I have many to agree. I lost the love for the game. So I left it. You must have a love and passion for the game/sport. Pursuing a sport for money will only peak you out early. When you pursue a sport for this reason, you are cheating someone else who really has a passion for the game, but may lack the abilities that you have. It is important to plan your future. I have helped many students and athletes to refocus, plan and pursue their future. I have had students who had given up on life and their future but after recruiting, coaching, motivating, mentoring, pushing and helping them get into college, they now have a complete new life.

Planning what you want to do is the key to the start of a lifelong success within that sport and subject area. Finding what major (subject area of study) is also just as important as the sport you choose to pursue a career in. If you are human, I hope we all are (smile), your body will experience wear and tear as you get older. At one point in time in your life, you as an athlete will have to have something to depend on other than depending on a sport that will not always be around. This is why I coach and mentor athletes to pursue an academic career as well as a sports career. You can choose one that you are passionate about and that career will carry you; and also if you choose to have a family later on in life. It should the breadwinner for you and your family. If you get injured or chose to retire, you will have something to fall back on. Scholarships are based on academics as well as your athletic abilities. Your academics are more important. If you do not pass and meet testing requirements, you will not be able to pursue your dream. It is important for any high school athlete to take your academic studies seriously, early, starting in your elementary years. More so in your middle school years. Coaches and recruiters look at your GPA (Grade Point Average). Some colleges do not consider you if your GPA do not meet their standards.

## When the Thrill is Gone:
## You Must Have Love for the Game

**W**HEN THE THRILL IS GONE: YOU MUST HAVE LOVE FOR THE GAME. When you lose the love for the game, the game is over. Quitting is the best choice. You can ask yourself this question: "Should I pursue something I do not like? Is it fair to my teammates and coaches who have love for the game? Is going pro the right thing to do if I do not love the game?" Trust me, your attitude and performance will show whether you're happy or sad. For example, I ran track all of my young teenage years up until high school graduation. I became burned out. I peeked my game and did not accept any college scholarships because I lost the love for the sport and did not want to pursue running after high school. I was great in it and had chances of getting some full scholarships but I did not pursue them because I lost the love for the game. It is like going into a new marriage or a new relationship and you do not feel the same way the spouse of significant other feels. There are two separate feelings involved and the more you try to make it work, to go with the flow, or cover it up, the truth will come out. Shame, embarrassment, or conflict will be the result if you do not make a conscious decision to be truthful with yourself, your family (mom, dad, or guardian), your teammates, and your coach. Then you should pursue something that will make you happy. By doing this, your performance will soar and you will be able to reach the highest potential you can reach.

# Experience #13

HOME GUEST

For the Struggling Athlete & Coach.
Middle School * High School * College * Pro Athlete & Coach

## Create Your Own Identity

CREATE YOUR OWN INDENTITY (*individuality, uniqueness, distinctiveness, self, character, personality*). Although you look up to pro and/or high school athletes, it is important to establish your own identity. Create "the you" in you. It is ok to look up to and idolize them, but only to idolize in a way that they serve only as positive examples; and so that you can become great or as popular as they are. But through your own identity, do not copy, **just be who you are.** This is why it is important to work hard, put in extra practices, off-season practices and camps, off-season leagues, camp programs, individual help from professional coaches who know the game and what they're talking about.

*Where they are going may not be where you may end up, so make sure you create "the you" in you and "JUST DO YOU".*

In looking to those who are ahead of you is not the time to try to be just like them. You want to be like yourself but learn from what it took, or is taking to get where they are, or where they are going. Where they are going may not be where you may end up, so make sure you **create "the you"** in you and **"JUST DO YOU"**. You can never go wrong just being yourself (Just Doing You). This is the best you can do when you do you. The key in just being you, is the power to know that you can get better and better, and better and better to the point where others will be looking up to you. You will then become idolized. I have had the opportunity of being looked up to and idolized because of my leadership and awards received while playing sports. People used to ask me "how does it feel to be popular"? I replied by answering, "I really don't think about it. I just work hard and do my best". This is a great way to be humble while creating "the you" in you—your own identity. Through my coaching and mentorship I have had the opportunity of working with a young man by the name of Torrey. He's headed for greatness. I say he's headed for greatness because he's putting in the work and he's determined to win on and off the field. He is a very smart student as well as athlete. He has a 3.2 grade point average on a 4.0 scale and has received awards and Division 1 college offers. I am very proud of him. I am also coaching and mentoring another young man by the name of Asa. He is in the eighth grade and since I have been working with him, he is now determined and has established his own identity. He is determined to make it. He has also made the honor roll and continue to strive for success. I also work with this young man by the name of Everett. He is my nephew. I am very proud of him. He has high hopes and dreams of becoming a basketball player in college one day, and he also loves to draw. He is motivated and has a high determination to win, and through establishing his own positive identity, he's on his way. His sister, Katyra is striving for the same success but she is striving through her academics and though her love to dance, read and draw. I am very proud of what they all are becoming. I also work with all of these

*Don't judge a book by its cover. If you do you may miss out on your entire promising future.*

and others through my non-profit center called, "The Purpose Center, Inc." in Houston, Texas. I help children and youth to reach their dreams and purpose who have given up hope or just do not have the finances, resources, motivation, or determination to do it themselves. Especially those in the inner-city and are less fortunate to get the help they need to succeed. I help them by academically tutoring, mentoring, counseling, and coaching them. This Center runs strictly off donations and monetary gifts.

Remember it is not what the person who helps you look like, but what is on the inside of that person that counts. Do not make judgments and decisions based on what a person looks like or by their gender. I am a woman and I coach and mentor more young men and men than young ladies and women. I teach that it does not matter who coaches, mentors, or helps you, what matters is that they know the game, what they are talking about, and have a desire and passion to help you to the end. Do not judge a book by its cover. If you do, you may miss out on your entire promising future.

Creating your own identity means you must dig deep within yourself and bring out only the best positive qualities you have. Don't worry about what people think or say about you. Just do the best you can. This works in academics too. You have to start thinking on a higher level than "all I gotta' do is pass my classes and I'm straight." This is not good enough. This is not good enough because you are not reaching for the highest potential you can do. You are settling for the ordinary and that will only get you an ordinary future. But to think on a high level of faith, determination, and conquering the impossible in your life to win will get you an extraordinary future. For example, take a step higher from the ordinary mindset and goal from saying "I'm going to college" to "I'm going to graduate from college". This is the level of faith to believe beyond the ordinary to conquering the impossible in your life. Another example is, "My parents didn't finish school, so all I gotta' do is just pass and I'll get my diploma" to "My parents didn't finish school, so I'm going to break the barrier and graduate top of my class from college".

It is important as a coach, teacher, and/or parent to help the athletes and students create their own identities. You are their leader and they are looking up to you. I can remember years ago in my teaching and coaching career, I have had the opportunity to teach one of the most popular and most famous pro basketball players in the NBA today, Kendrick Perkins who plays for the

Oklahoma Thunder. I can remember him walking into my classroom and having to bend his head down in order to walk into my classroom. I still smile at the thought. I would always encourage him to be the best he can be, although I'm sure he already knew that inside, but me as a teacher did my part to instill encourage and motivation within him. I always believed that he was going to be a pro basketball player. He would listen as I spoke to him and agreed. He would say, "I gotcha' Ms. Franklin." I still smile at the thought. He was a well-mannered young man. Athletes and students, it is important to listen to those teachers, coaches, parents, and mentors that are placed in your life to encourage, push and help you get to the level that you need to be. Teachers and coaches it is important to mentor and motivate your students and athletes to be the best they can be and not tear them down. You cannot take it for granted that they already are encouraged and confident within themselves. Your words may be the right words they need at that right moment. There are times when these important nuggets are taken for granted, and as a result, at times, have been very detrimental for the athlete and for the student (major shut down, suicide, crimes, gangs, etc.). I am so grateful to have taught Kendrick Perkins, and look forward to one day seeing him again, and letting him know how proud I am of him and all of his accomplishments he has made not only as an athlete but also as a leader. I challenge more athletes to step up and become successful just like Kendrick. If you as a coach or a teacher have an athlete you know that have made it famous or have made great success, I challenge you to encourage more athletes and students to be successful like them. Kendrick is one of the many that I have had the opportunity to motivate, speak words of encouragement, and instill spiritual guidance in while in my class. I hope you will do the same and keep the chain going on. It is much needed in the school district. Students and athletes need to know that there is someone who cares and believes in them. **You are the chosen one so do the best you can and make everyday count.**

## *Parents, You Are A Part of the Process*

**P**ARENTS, YOU ARE A PART OF THE PROCESS. Dedicated parents of an athlete are the athlete's biggest cheer leader(s). In fact, nobody can beat a supporting, dedicated, and devoted parent. Their constant chants are, "I know you're ganna' be a star!" "My baby's gon' make it pro one day and gon' make momma or daddy proud." "I'm your biggest fan." "Top colleges gon' pick

> *YOU ARE IMPORTANT AND YOU PLAY A VITAL ROLE IN YOUR CHILD'S FUTURE. YOU ARE NOT LEFT OUT.*

you up and you gon' make it big one day." "You're the best!" And the list goes on and on and means more than you can ever know to your child/athlete. Just one loving word of encouragement can change a child's life. Just one encouraging word can keep a child from committing suicide or turning to gangs and clicks for acceptance and love. So please do not think that you are over doing it if you are a parent who practices this with your child on a daily basis. It is needed.

There are also cases where many parents and single parents who work long hours or are incarcerated and do not get a chance to go to your child's games. There are many athletes who do not have the support of their parents or guardians at all for whatever reason. As a result the child/athlete travels alone. Feels alone. Struggles alone. Hurt alone. Celebrate alone. They make it big alone. It is hard when the parent is never available to support the child/athlete's games and or sporting events—especially when you are able and available to support. Excuses never win. You cannot be a part of the **process** if you have this type of attitude. Now on the other hand, if you are a hard working parent and support is impossible due to a demanding job or work schedule, I can understand. But throughout the years and seasons of your child's sporting life and career, you should have made time to make some games or sporting events. Your child needs it.

There are also many cases where the parent(s) were too laid back in the past and now the talented child/athlete is getting much attention and looks from coaches and recruiters; even those at an early middle school age. So now you back up and take on the guilt trip. This should not be so. You should feel guilty but you do not have to stay feeling guilty. Everybody (parent(s) or guardian) makes mistakes. Nobody is perfect. You can make a turnaround now. You are not left out of the picture during the athlete's career and recruiting **process** and choices. Your child still needs you. You should at this point go to your child/children/son/daughter and ask for their forgiveness and try to make amends. Fathers, if this is you, and you have been missing out of the child/children/son/daughter's life and/or sporting life, you should go and ask for their forgiveness, go and supporting them (may have to take it slow), and give them time to open up and receive you as God helps mend your relationship, either together or back together.

Most times the recruiting **process** and choices are between the athlete and coach. But I want you as the parent or guardian to know that you are just as an important factor during the process than the coach and the athlete. You do not have to continue feeling guilty of not supporting your child/athlete because of all those years you missed supporting them. You can make a turn-a-round today and get it right with them as I stated before. Let them know you are sorry and make a conscious decision that you are going to support them from here on out. If you work and making the games are impossible, take some vacation time, or take a day off (if possible), or take advantage of the time you have off and spend time with them. You will never know how this goes a long way in your child's life. I remember when I was in middle school; there was a time when my mom's job became very demanding to the point where she could not come at times during the week. She would make time. She made time on the weekends when we had games, track meets, tournaments, etc. This is what you will have to do. You do your best. You may not be able to make it during the week, but weekend games or track meets or tournaments are just as good. Even if you are not able to make the games during the week, your encouraging voice, motivation when they get home or after the game is a must and is acceptable. It shows them that you care and are concerned. Believe me, children/athletes understand when you have to work to take care of them. But what bothers them is when you do not ask them how their game was? Did they win? How did they do? Tell them they're doing a great job, how proud you are of them, and how you believe in them; and tell them they are going to be something big one day, etc. Encouragement goes a long way. Love goes longer. Fussing at them will never win. I understand, as I am a coach too and work with young people, that you have to push or discipline them in order that they may get stronger, get better, grow or grow up. But cursing and yelling at them does nothing but make them afraid and hinders their progress or ability to succeed within that sport and in life. There was a time as a child that my dad pushed me very hard, in fact too hard, and expected too much out of me to a degree that he was living his life through me that made it very hard to please him. He yelled and cursed as he trained me at times too hard to a point where it became unbearable, and reaching my full potential was out of the question. My success went down, my attitude became very negative and rebellious, and our relationship was at a no win situation. I ended up not going to college in that sport that I had worked so hard throughout the years to pursue. I ended up going for another sport instead. He and I now have made amends after years later; and have talked about the past and have put it behind us. He now understands how I felt and sees where he could have done better. No one is perfect, he was learning as a coach and as a father. So parents/guardians please, it is important as a coach and parent to watch the way you constantly yell, put your child/athlete down, and make them feel less of a person. You will push them away to maybe something more detrimental than you expected.

Children/youth are not strong like adults. They are still developing mentally, emotionally, and physically. You have to learn how to give and take. You <u>give</u> discipline, and then you love on them and let them know that you are only helping them to get better—that is <u>taking</u>. You are not tearing them down; you are always building them up.

Also, reward your child. Take them for ice cream or take them to do something they like. Spend time with them. Not what you want to do, but what they want to do. Or, if negotiated you and them can do something you both like to do. This adds to the motivating process so when they get out on the court or field, they are motivated to do their best and not feel as if they can never please you, or they're so afraid they cannot perform to the best of their ability. I hope you understand what I am telling you. This is a serious subject that **ALL** parents should to take note and apply to their lives.

I counsel parents, parents and their children, and youth alone or together, and the first thing the child or youth says as we are all meeting is, "Why ya'll always got somethin' negative to say?"

Or, "Why ya'll always at work and never try to make my games?" Or, "Why ya'll don't ask me how was my day or how did I do in the game or at school?" Or, "How's my grades?" Or, "All ya'll do is fuss at me." Or, "All daddy do is fuss and curse at me." Or, "Momma you ain't never got nothin' good to say." These are just some of the things that are said. There are many more. This should not be so. This must be changed if you want to win your child/youth and help them to reach their full potential in life. And also, to have a loving, close, and trusting relationship with your child/youth. When you do these things, you can get anything out of them and they will feel comfortable to talk to you; and to do their best in anything they apply themselves to do—because they now know that you are with them and <u>believe in them</u>.

Your presence is important and appreciated. Your words of encourage is important and appreciated. Your practice visits and pick-ups are important and appreciated. Your late after the game pick-ups are important and appreciated. You getting your child/athlete to practice on time are important and appreciated. You showing up at the games and supporting your child/athlete and the team are important and appreciated. You introducing yourself and interacting with the coach are important and appreciated. You helping your child academically (*grades, taking proper test needed for college, making "A's", and pushing them to stay on top of things) are* important and appreciated. You helping the child/athlete make important college decisions, recruiting choices and decisions are important and appreciated. Your yells of encouragement at the games or track meets are important and appreciated. And, all of the sacrifices you make on a daily basis as well as through the good times and stressful times of getting what your child needs, and where they need to be are important and appreciated. All of these examples are the **process** for your child/son/daughter/athlete getting to his or her successful, promising future. **YOU ARE IMPORTANT AND YOU PLAY A VITAL ROLE IN YOUR CHILD'S/SON'S/DAUGHTER'S FUTURE. YOU ARE NOT LEFT OUT,** and you do not have to feel left out when someone else who is chosen comes in and helps with your child, son or daughter because they too are a vital part of their promising future and purpose. You never know how powerful your prayers are. God will send you help because of your prayers, and their help will be rewarding but only if you share the space and allow them to do their part/assignment without feeling inferior, afraid, intimidated, or again, left out.

Kids/youth often say, "Parents just don't understand". I can agree both ways. If you are a parent that has never played sports and do not desire it at all, they are right you don't understand. But if you are a parent who has played the sport and have a love for the sport or game, you are among the few who do. I encourage those parents to relax who do not play sports and do not have a passion for the game. It is not a no win situation for you. You can still win. Let me tell you how you can win, you can win by making sure you are supportive of your child's games, academics, and being their emotional outlet when they need you.

You as the parent are a major part of The Locker Room Experience. When your part is done, your child will feel better before games and while preparing for their games in the locker room with their teammates and coaches. There is a balance. If the home life is not right or if there is trouble and conflicted situations going on in the home, it will affect the child/athlete's performance and attitude; resulting in emotional attacks and battles, team conflicts, disobedience, hatred, jealous of other parents supporting their child, and so on. So, please know how important your role is.

You may be a parent of a professional athlete. This also applies to you although you may already have enough money, so long work hours may not be your downfall, but there are many others. Many athletes, we have heard in the TV news as well as in the newspapers, how some are more traumatized by fame, fortune, struggles from bad habits and not knowing how to handle bad relationships. These types of athletes are in need of a supporting family, friends, teammates, and coaching staff. I'm sure there are many who do give the support that are needed, but there are still few who do not. As a result, the tabloids which are most times not true, turn out to be true—athletes committing suicide, athletes killing one another, athletes killing their girlfriends/boyfriends or husbands/wives and then themselves, or athletes overdosing, athletes ending their lives due to excessive alcohol, etc. This should not be so. There should be support groups along with annual workshops and seminars on how to handle emotions, struggles, and fortune that each athlete must take while being on the team. When an athlete is taught how to handle their emotions and deal with their struggles, such situations that come up in life will be overcome victoriously by the experience they will have received in how to handle such situations.

## Huddle up!: *The Motivating Experience*

HUDDLE UP!: THE MOTIVATING EXPERIENCE. LOCKER ROOM EXPERIENCE EXCERSISES YOU CAN DO WITH YOU'RE YOUR TEAMMATES before and after practice and before each game:

1. When you come into the locker room, you come in with an attitude of, "we gon' win" and not an attitude of, "there's no way we gon' beat them".

2. Huddle in a circle together. Grab each other's hand or lay your hand on the other teammates shoulder as a group. (You can do this either before you put on your uniforms or afterwards, right before you leave out of the locker room).

3. Tell and tell the teammate on your right side how much you appreciate them.

4. Turn and tell the teammate on your left side how much you appreciate them.

5. Find one person and pump them up by encouraging that person to play their "A Game".

6. Huddle with the coach and tell the coach an encouraging word.

7. Come up with a motivating chant that everybody will yell to the top of their lungs to get everybody motivated for the game as you all leave to go out to the court, track, or field.

**You are a team.** You should always remember that if one teammate is down, the entire team is down. If one teammate wins, the entire team wins. **YOU ARE ONE**. There are no big "I's" or "Little Me's" everyone carries their own weight. One person cannot carry the weight of the entire team, or the team puts everything on one person to perform all of the tasks needed to win the game. The team wins by everybody's effort.

HOME    GUEST

For the Struggling Athlete & Coach.
Middle School • High School • College • Pro Athlete & Coach

# Experience #16

## The Recruiting Process and Experience: Learn the Technique of the Sport

THE RECRUITING PROCESS AND EXPERIENCE: LEARN THE TECHNIQUE OF THE SPORT. Have you ever dreamed of becoming famous or dreamed of being a pro athlete? The only thought was going through your mind was, "man, I wish I was a pro athlete so I can be rich and make my momma proud!" Well, I am here to help you get through the process in order to make your dream come true. It will not come over night. You must put time, hard work, and dedication in it. Nothing comes easy in life. You gotta' get out there and do it. The process is called, "Recruiting". Yes recruiting. Now days it's all about networking and getting your name out there so coaches, scouts and recruiters can have an opportunity to know who you are and see what kind of skills you got. You must sell yourself. Recruiting early is important. You should begin recruiting early, such as, in Middle School. Some may say start in the beginning of your freshmen year in high school, but I disagree. I believe you should begin while you are in middle school, preferably in the seventh grade. I always tell the athletes, "you are not baby's, it's time to grow up". Starting at this time is essential to helping the young athlete to grow up and began to think about and to take their future seriously. I remember when I was in middle school. I was very well known and popular in sports. I won many awards—certificates, numerous of first place ribbons, metals, trophy's, and was asked by the Jesse Owens Games to carry the Jesse Owens torch to open up the Jesse Owens Games in Los Angeles, California. I did not get there

> *I could not think like a baby, I had to think like an athlete with a promising future.*

over night. I had to work hard be dedicated to the sport. I was one of the captains on the cross country, volleyball, basketball, and track & field team; and I never lost a race in track & field along with being very popular. I also traveled all over the United States and ran in the Junior Olympics (TAC) and in AAU track & field for over ten years; and was also very popular in that. My point in sharing this is to say that in my middle school years, there were high school coaches and college scouts and recruiters pursuing and looking at me. I could not think like a baby, I had to think like a young lady—an athlete with a promising future. I had to think about what I wanted to do. It was important for me to decide what sport I wanted to pursue because I was the one who had to do it and be happy with it. This is why I say it is time to grow up. You cannot put everything on your mom, dad or guardian. It was time for me to decide what sport to be the main sport to focus all my attention on considering I had four sports to choose from (Cross Country, Volleyball, Basketball, and Track & Field, also played tennis and softball but not in school). If you play multiple sports like, football, basketball, volleyball, baseball, cross country, softball, soccer, tennis, softball, track and field, cheerleading, dance, etc., it is obvious to know that it is not smart to pursue all of them at the same time for scholarships and for a career. They are all absolutely too many to pursue all together. You will

*The recruiting process is simple if you follow and be persistent with it.*

have to choose one, maybe two for your career. Not that it cannot be done, because I believe all things are possible if you believe. I have seen some athletes do football and baseball or Volleyball and track and Field in college, not many, but it can be done. College sports are not like high school sports. They have triple the amount of games than an average high school. Also traveling is an added feature. Although you may travel to different schools and maybe one or two surrounding towns and/or cities, it is nothing like the travel you will do during your college years within that particular sport with two and three games per week along with tournaments and conference games—including rigorous practices. It will become tiresome. And there will be challenging moments. You may even become burned out, especially with more than one sport year round. There again, it can be done, but I do not encourage it.

The recruiting process is simple if you follow and be persistent with it. Every athlete wants to be recruited and to go to a Division I, prestige school. This comes with a price. Most athletes do not make it to Division I schools because they do not have the help they need to get there, the right grades and/or GPA, low SAT and/or ACT test scores, failure to do research and recruit schools and put their name out there, failure to put in the time, failure to listen when help does come their way, and lack the confidence to believe in their talent(s) and just do it. As a freshman in high school you should be doing as much networking as possible. You should be targeting as many schools as possible as you can to potential colleges or universities to attend.

You should not blame your high school coach for your success. It is true that most high school coaches **do not** have the time to do **ALL** of the recruiting for each athlete. They have their family and own personal life to tend to. As bad as you may not want to hear this I have to say it, but high school coaches are not responsible for doing **ALL** of your recruiting for you. Yes, if you are a junior or a senior, they are responsible for helping you as an athlete to get recruited, but they are not responsible to do **ALL** of the work and <u>you do nothing</u>. You as the athlete should be in constant relationship and communication with your coach. You should let him or her know what your future plans are, where you would like to go to school, what are the best options for you as an athlete for that particular sport, and ask how and what are some things you can do to improve your athletic ability in order to be in position or a prospect to receive a scholarship.

I am going to give you a chart, an outlined plan showing how you should be networking (making contacts) and recruiting each year. It's all about networking—getting your name out there and showing what you got (recruiting DVD-video showing you in action in your sport) and making potential contacts. Here are the charted plans:

## Your Freshman Year:

1. **PLAN:** Go get a sheet of paper or writing pad and a pen or pencil. Write down all of the schools (colleges/universities) where you would like to play sports. Do not try to be perfect in this. This is only a rough list that will be narrowed down later.

    Finding an **academic major (a career)** you want to pursue alongside of your sports career is the next thing you want to do as you plan. Remember, sports is not everything. You will not be playing sports for the rest of your life. You're going to need a back bone, something to fall back on especially if you get injured, retire from the sport, or for other reasons. **On another sheet of paper or on the same writing pad, write down each of the academic majors (careers) you would like to pursue.** You may have more than one. If you do, this means you will have what is called a major and a minor or double major. You are not entitled to have more than one major. For example, you may want to own your own business one day so choosing Business Administration as your major would be appropriate. Another example, you may enjoy mechanical things or enjoy working with electronics so Engineering (Mechanical Engineering or Electrical Engineering) would be appropriate for this choice. And the list goes on. If you are still undecided, you still have time but do not take too long because this will be a part of the deciding factor as you choose the college or university you want to attend; either for a sports scholarship, walk-on, or for academic scholarships.

2. **RESEARCH: Search the Internet.** Now that you have written out your college list of schools and have decided on an academic major *(if not, there's still time)*, it is time to do your research by visiting each of the colleges/universities website on the internet to see if they ALL have the qualities you are looking for, both sports and academics. The two work together.

3. **ACTION: Prepare a letter of interest.** The internet has hundreds of templates you can use for this. Your letter should not be lengthy. It should be straight to the point. You may ask, "Why do I have to plan, do research, and

prepare a letter of Interest already, I'm only a freshman?" I will first say, good question. But to answer your question "it is important to start early and prepare so that scouts and recruits can start watching you. If you wait, it may be too late. They may choose someone else because they did not know you exist or were interested."

**Send each school a sports schedule** of the sports you would like for them to come to. You may not be able to visit each school, so inviting them to come watch you play (participate) would be just as good.

**Go to Camps.** You must participate in as many camps as you can so that recruiters and scouts can see what you got. Many times great athletes have missed out on attending top D 1 (Division 1) schools because they did not attend camps. No one knew who they were. You may not be able to attend all of them, but you should try your best to attend as many as you can. Also, when you do attend these camps, you should make sure that you do not clown around and waste your time, your money or your parent's money by not taking them seriously. This is the time to show what you got, to prove that you have what it takes to compete on the college level.

## Your Sophomore Year:

1.  **PLAN:** Now that you have written out your college list, have written out your academic list and decided your academic major, now it is time to narrow your list of schools down. Cross out the schools that do not have your sports or academic major. You may have come across a school that has your sports but does not have your academic major; you should cross that school out. Or, you may come cross a school that has your academic major but does not have your sports; you still should not choose this school. You want to choose a school that has both. Trust me there are plenty of schools (colleges/universities) to choose from.

2.  **RESEARCH:** Surfing the internet can be challenging at times, so if you are struggling in this area you should get help from your parents, teachers, or school officials. Do a more in-depth search and narrow your schools down to about ten schools.

3.  **ACTION:** You should have already prepared a letter of interest on last year (your freshman year). Now it is time to send another letter to those schools that you have narrowed your list down to. It is time to contact those coaches, scouts, and recruiters again either by mail, email, or you may even prepare a college visit on your own. There is no limit in doing this. You should send as many

and as much as possible. Be careful to follow NCAA rules before doing this.

You may also talk to other athletes that are trying to do the same thing you are doing. You can get some tips and encouragement this way as well. Maybe you can work together.

You must continue to compete and work hard while continuously doing your research.

## Your Junior Year:

1. **PLAN/RESEARCH:** If you have done your research right, you should by now have decided what school (college/university) you want to attend. As I have a stated earlier in the book, it is not a good idea to wait until your senior year to decide what college or pro team you would like to attend. You should have already done your planning, research, and recruiting before now. If you have not, surely it is not too late, you can still decide but your work may be harder due to the fact that there are other goals that should have been reached before your senior year. If you are deciding whether or not to go pro, it is a good idea to get a good recruiting agent, find a good coach who has excellent networking with pro teams and pro coaches. Sometimes it is who you know and word of

mouth. But not always. Planning and preparation is important not slothfulness. Timing and prayer is always needed.

2. **ACTION:** All letters of interest should be out there and you should be receiving camp invitations, surveys, and admissions information from Division I, II, or III coaches. Continuous contacting is the key and attending as many camps as possible are a must. There is no limit in doing this. You should contact as much as possible. Be careful to follow NCAA rules before doing this.

You may also talk to other athletes that are trying to do the same thing you are doing. You can get some tips and encouragement this way as well.

You must continue to compete and work hard while continuously doing your research.

You must remember academic testing is very important. Coaches want to see if you can meet the standards in your books as well as in the sport. So taking the SAT and the ACT test are essential. This is important and will determine what schools will pick you up. If your test does not meet the proper standards, you may not be picked up by very many, if any at all.

## Your Senior Year:

1. **PLAN/RESEARCH:** This should be the peak of the recruiting process for you. You should now plan to hear from coaches and recruiters. They are now able to call you except on quiet, dead, or evaluation periods. You should be on constant watch. You should also have a list of the schools that you are interested in attending, and a list of who you have already been in contact with.

2. **ACTION:** Now is the time to narrow down your list to the school or pro team that is the best fit for you. This is why it is important not to depend on one school, but have more than one choice to choose from.

   Now that this is your senior year, you can now take official visits from recruiters, scouts, and coaches. There is a difference between official and unofficial visits. Official visits are where schools may pay for your transportation, food, and lodging. This does not always apply to the family that wants to come and support, it only applies to the student athlete. Athlete are only allowed 5 official visits to Division I and Division II also called, D-I and D-II. If the athlete does not want to take Division I official visits, they may take as many official visits to Division II schools, but is disqualified from playing Division I sports. This is important information to remember so be wise in your decision making. Parents, guardians, and/or coaches your assistance is needed in assisting your son or daughter in this matter.

If official visits are taken by the student athlete, more than likely you will receive an offer from one of the schools. Please take your time and consider this step very carefully. This is your future you are talking about. Most coaches will give you time to think about the decision you are making because they understand that it is a life changing step that should be considered by you and your parent or guardian with care and not taken lightly. Please do not consider a school because your friend or relative is attending that school. Although it is a good idea to go off to a school and be with someone you know, but their choice may not be the best choice in terms of sports and/or academics for you, or vice versa. If both of your choices line up right and everything falls in line for the both of your careers and futures, I say go with it. You have my best regards.

Remember this is the competitive process and the decision can get very intense. So take your time. Prayerfully make your choice as best as you can.

**HERE ARE SOME SPECIFIC QUESTIONS AND ANSWERS FOR YOU AS YOU ARE ON YOUR RECRUITING VENUE:**

**QUESTIONS & ANSWERS:**

**QUESTION:**

What are 10 things I should include in my letter of interest?

**ANSWER:**

1. Make sure that your name is visible.

2. Make sure you have an accurate <u>point of contact</u>.

3. Make sure you get to the point and do not become wordy. If the letter is too long and wordy, it may not be looked at.

4. Be confident and not confused in your letter and state exactly **<u>why</u>** and **<u>what</u>** you want. You want the coach/recruiter to know what and why you are interested and are the best pick for them.

5. Your GPA, ACT/SAT scores, and any honors and awards you may have from your school (academic, athletic, club, camp, and any combines) is important to add.

6. Add what high school or college (if going pro) you are attending.

7. Do not start your letter with "To Whom it May Concern". It is not good to start your letter off with this statement. You want to do your research and find out what the head coach's name is or the assistant coach who is recruiting

you. It makes your letter personal and they know you have been doing your research and you are defiantly interested.

8. Writing bad things about your high school or college (if going pro) coach, coaching staff, and team (season record, etc.) are prohibited.

9. Add a recruiting link for the coach to link to for further research about your athletic abilities, progress, and highlight video.

10. Do not address the letter or send it to the wrong school. This is embarrassing. Make sure if you are emailing the letter, that you look at the address you are sending the letter to first before sending it. Also the same if you are mailing the letter.

**QUESTION:**

**What should I say on a phone call with a college coach and/or recruit?**

**ANSWER:**

It is good to listen to them and wait until they ask you a question. Never talk too much. Keep your answers short and straight to the point.

**QUESTION:**

**I'm not being recruited. What are 2 things I need to know so I don't get overlooked?**

**ANSWER:**

Get your information out there by doing your research and by sending your letters out to schools (colleges/universities).

**QUESTION:**

**How Long Should I Wait to Follow Up On a Previous Call?**

**ANSWER:**

Not long. Your follow up should be immediate.

**QUESTION:**

**What should be my Game Plan For Success?**

**ANSWER:**

Good grades. Good conduct. Constantly train. Go to camps for improvement. Decide on the school of your choice. Send them a letter of interest. Do not give up!

**QUESTION:**

**At What Division Level Can I Compete?**

**ANSWER:**

You and your coach will have to decide on that based on your athletic ability, progress, and success within that particular sport.

**QUESTION:**

**How do I get eligible for the NCAA rules?**

**ANSWER:**

Good grades, make sure you did not play pro sports before college, follow the rules, and register. You may also ask your high school if you are uncertain about the NCAA Rules. They should have all of the information you need. You may also visit NCAA's website.

## WHAT YOU MUST DO IN ORDER TO GET RECRUITED:

1. Maintain a good GPA and get tutoring for those subjects you are having trouble in.

2. Set goals to improve and achieve your athletic and physical ability.

3. Stay out of trouble, respect everyone, and be a leader by keeping a positive attitude with those around you.

4. Learn the rules of the game and study NCAA rules.

5. Visit websites online and leave your information where they are required.

6. Send out letters of Interest.

7. Check on the progress of colleges you sent out letters to on a daily basis.

8. Must have a highlight video of your games.

## 8 IMPORTANT THINGS TO KNOW ABOUT PREPARING & RECEIVING FINANCIAL AID:

1. Know where to go to fill out your financial Aid (FAFSA).

2. Opportunities come with great grades (academics).

3. Don't wait too late to start your Financial Aid.

4. Complete your Financial Aid before the due date.

5. Talk to your coaches and counselor about financial aid in advance.

6. Know that you may not be limited to a full scholarship, so make sure you are connected with the recruiter/coach to know what type of scholarship they are offering you.

7. If you're not limited to a full scholarship, know how much and what type of financial aid to ask for. (Pell Grants and/or Loans, etc.).

8. Check with your school counselor on a daily basis for updates and important questions and answers you may have.

## 10 SIGNS TO KNOW THAT YOU ARE BEHIND ON RECRUITING:

1. Sitting down on the couch, watching others do all the work to get recruited.

2. Not putting in work (training and going to camps).

3. You do not have a highlight video of your games.

4. You do not have letters sent out or ready.

5. Bad grades and bad conduct.

6. You have a don't care attitude of whatever.

7. Listening to people who cannot help you.

8. Not taking your future seriously.

9. Listening to people who do not like or have sports knowledge.

10. Getting recruiting advice from those who are not experienced.

## 8 THINGS NOT TO SAY TO A RECRUITER/COACH:

1. I'm the best one you'll ever pick, so pick me.

2. You need me.

3. Do not pester (bother) the recruiter/coach as they are still in the recruiting process or looking at you.

4. Do not ask how much money they can offer you right away. There is a process and order. After you know that the coach is interested in offering you a scholarship, then

| | |
|---|---|
| | you may inquire about scholarship and financial Aid (If needed) opportunities. |
| 5. | Where's the contract? You should never ask if there is a contract involved. The coach has the ability to offer you a scholarship and he or she does not. Allow them to let you know what is involved first before adding any additional information you are not sure of. |
| 6. | I'm not sure of myself, but I think... |
| 7. | I like your school but I'm in love with another school. |
| 8. | Not taking your future seriously. |

**You must learn the techniques of the sport you are pursuing.** It makes it easier when you master the sport that you are pursuing.

You must also take your school work, homework, tests, and GPA seriously as well. During my time in school, they had just passed a law "No pass no play" rule. If an athlete did not pass his or her studies (classes) he or she could not play or continue to play in sports, band, choir, debate team, dance team, cheer leader, etc. No matter how good they were. It is the same today. If you do not pass your classes, you cannot play sports or others, no matter how good or talented you are. This rule should be taken very seriously. It may be the deciding factor to whether or not a college coach will give you a scholarship over another athlete because their grades are much better than yours are and they feel they can trust them academically better than you. So take your studies seriously and do your best; and be on your "A Game" everyday on and off the field, court, or track.

---

**Here Are Points That Will Help you Understand the Recruiting Process and What College Recruits look for:**

1. Take your grades seriously. This should begin when you first start school.

2. Start early with making the honor roll to boost your GPA for high school. Your seventh grade middle school years should be your start.

3. As an athlete, bring your "A Game" in every sport you pursue. Encourage others to do the same.

4. **Your freshman year in high school:** Begin to think about what major you want to pursue in college.

5. **Your freshman year in high school:** Think about what college you would like to go to and have the major you want to pursue.

6. **Your freshman year in high school:** Do your research for that particular school to see what they have to offer, and if they have the major you want to pursue.

7. **Your freshman year in high school:** If you are involved in multiple sports, it is important to narrow one or two of the sports you would like to pursue in college. Now that you have done your research on the college and whether

or not it has your major, now is time to see if they have the sports you would like to pursue and obtain a scholarship in. All of these work together. You do not want to pursue a college that has your sport, but do not have your major. Because, remember what I said earlier, you will not be playing sports all of your life, your body will get older and will come to a point where you will eventually have to retire or you may get injured and you will need to have something to fall back on. Your major should be able to carry you along with other types of investments and plans.

8. **Your Freshman Year in high school:** You should start sending them a letter of interest and DVD's that show your level of skills in action within that sport to those various schools to let them know that you are interested. Also you want to make sure you are specific in what your classification is, GPA, and briefly speak about your awards and accomplishments.

9. **Your Sophomore Year in high school:** Compete on the high school level, take your academics seriously by making good grades (honor roll is always a great thing to strive for), take classes that are going to push you, do not just settle for classes that are way too easy in order to pass. The higher your classes are, the higher your GPA and class rank will rise.

10. **Your Junior Year in high school:** Begin taking your SAT and ACT tests. You should have received letters and/or emails from college recruiters by now if you've done your homework. If not, go back to the drawing board and send letters of interest and DVD's out to more colleges. You may have to send letters out to those you did not expect to send to, be realistic. You may not meet the Division I standards, so pursuing a Division II is not bad, go for it and get what you need. Also, you may have to resort to a Division III level. This is not bad either. There have been great athletes who came out of these levels and still made it big. It is in your drive, determination, and will to win in life and not to lose and give up. You cannot be lazy or wait on others. You must step up and talk to your coach, school counselor, and mentor if you have one and let them know your plans for your future and do not be shame to ask for help. That is what they are there for. They are there to help you and are willing to help.

11. **Your Senior year in high school:** You should have taken all of your test and gotten the score you need for the college of your choice, have already spoken or communicated in some way with the college recruiter or coach you are interested in to a degree of them either offering you scholarship. Your spring semester should be

> the deciding factor and preparation to leave for that college. I did not mention about prom and all the other senior stuff that are just as important, but this is most important. There is no greater feeling than to know that there is life and a college/university to call your own during this time. You can now sigh a sigh of relief <u>because you are now ready</u>.

Following these points early will help you far along than not doing anything at all and missing out on a rewarding future in pursuing the sport you are well qualified and able to excel in. So many athletes and young people miss their purpose and future because of lack of help and motivation to know they can do it. Through this book and guidance, "The Locker Room Experience", you will receive the truth and the guide you need to pursue your college and professional career you have been longing for.

## MAKING A HIGHLIGHT VIDEO:

It is important for every athlete to have a highlight video to show college and pro scouts and recruiters your skills. If you as an athlete plan to earn a scholarship, college coaches do not have the time nor do they have the money to travel to every athlete who sends them a letter of interest. They receive hundreds and some even thousands of letters and emails on a constant basis. They could not travel to all who are interested. This is why a highlight video is important for every athlete to take advantage of. I understand how hard it can be just to get a scout, recruiter or coach of a university to look your way. This is why I have started my own company that specializes in making Highlight Videos for the athlete. The company name is, **"SF Productions"** and if you are in need of a highlight video, I encourage you to visit my website: **www.sfproduction.net**. Highlight videos are not just for the middle school and high school athletes, it is also for pro athletes as well. Pro athletes use these videos if they are trying to move to another team, for personal resumes, and more. I strongly encourage you to take advantage of this service that I have offered. If you do not choose to, make sure you have other professional options that can and will help you.

## HIGHLIGHT VIDEOS SHOULD INCLUDE THE FOLLOWING:

In order for a highlight video to be effective and rewarding, it should consist of the following:

1.   **Should be kept short (no more than 5 minutes).** This video should do just what it says, "highlight" and not create a movie. It should show only your best skills in selected games you have played. First impressions mean everything. Coaches will spend very little time on each video so do not clutter your video with stuff that is ok. They do not need a long time to know whether or not you're the one they're looking for, so make it your best.

2. **Start with the best footage first.** Do not add just the ok in the beginning. You should start with nothing but the best.

3. **You must do research and know what each coach expects.** Each sport is different and should show only the footage that caters to your best skills and approaches. For example, baseball and softball should show only skills footage. Unlike basketball, football, and soccer should show plenty of game footage. You can see examples at www.sfproduction.net.

4. **Your video should be put with an online resume/letter of interest.** You should not send a coach/college a YouTube video or a DVD video. This would not be proper. You will need to send a highlight video that is properly formatted and placed on a trusted site that college coaches are going to trust. If your highlight video is emailed, it is still safe only if the coach can click one time on it and it takes them directly to your highlight, and not through numerous steps to get there. By doing this, it will discourage them from viewing your video further.

5. **Show all areas of skills you have.** For example, if you play basketball, you should not only show you shooting, you should also show that you are well rounded, like showing your defensive skills, your team assist skills, your ability to dribble skills as well. Coaches like to see if you are versatile and not just shooting all the time. This goes for every sport. I just used basketball as an example. Another

example is the sport of volleyball. Coaches do not only want to see how well you spike the ball, but they also want to see how well you set the ball (if that is your position), and also how well you play back row, front row or even the net in a defensive position. Try not to send unnecessary footage that will detour the coach from watching. They are not looking for show-offs, but athletes and team players who are versatile, and play different areas and do different moves and techniques.

6. **Your video intro makes a big difference.** You want to start your video with a short intro that will lead them into the highlights. Make sure you do not over-do it. It is only a short intro and not the body of the video.

7. **The quality of your video should be superb.** If the quality of your video is not up to par, you will want to take it somewhere and get it professionally done. If you are doing it yourself, you will want to make sure you read the instructions carefully on your camcorder or camera. Quality can make or break your chances of a once in a life-time opportunity if they are not recorded in a professional manner. Also, make sure you are visually seen. If you are not visually seen, make sure you add spot shadowing to point and/or highlight where you are in the video. This will help the coach/recruiter locate you easily. Just them knowing your number is not enough. They will need to

see where you are and what you are doing, whether you are out on the court, track, or field.

**FOR MORE INFO ON HOW TO PURCHASE YOUR HIGHLIGHT VIDEO, GO TO: www.sfproduction.net for purchasing prices and info.**

If you need more information on getting counseling and/or mentoring, go to: www.stephaniefranklinministries.org

If you need more information on how to get involved with programs that are geared to help your child academically, athletically (sports camps), and physical mentoring (weight issues), go to: www.thepurposecenter.org

If you are interested in getting personal training, strength training, agility, endurance, speed, and/or rehabilitation training, you may email: info@stephaniefranklinministries.com

# THE **LOCKER ROOM** *Experience*
**Epilogue:** *The Final Score*

The final score comes down to you. Are you going to push until the end? Or are you going to give up and weaken out? Only the strong survives. You must hang in there when the going gets tough. "The Locker Room Experience" allows the athlete and the coach to know what he or she needs to know about being a better athlete and coach. Nobody is perfect. There are always areas of improvement for the athlete and for the coach. What makes a great coach is the coach that will not give up on his or her team, they will look for areas of improvement for their team (workshops, team camps, accelerated practices, etc.). What makes a great athlete is an athlete who looks for ways for improvement, makes good grades their first priority, takes SAT/ACT testing seriously, faithful to their sport—coaching staff and teammates, and is humble and able to accept criticism where it is needed in order to better themselves.

"The Locker Room Experience" has been successful in helping the coach and athlete on all levels—emotional, moral, academic, financial, training, and recruiting.

# THE **LOCKER ROOM** *Experience*
## *My Recruiting Log*

On the lines below I have provided a recruiting log for you. You will joint down your process, progress, and goals toward recruiting.

---

**MONDAY**

_____

_____

_____

_____

_____

_____

_____

_____

_____

_____

_____

_____

_____

_____

_____

_____

_____

_____

_____

_____

_____

_____

_____

_____

**TUESDAY**

## WEDNESDAY

## THURSDAY

**FRIDAY**

# SATURDAY

**SUNDAY**

*My Practice Log*

Below is your practice log. This is your private personal log to document your practice success. Your improvements and areas where you are struggling to target and make it a goal to get better.

---

**MONDAY**

## TUESDAY

## WEDNESDAY

**THURSDAY**

# FRIDAY

**SATURDAY**

## SUNDAY

## EXTRA WRITING SPACE

# THE **LOCKER ROOM** *Experience*
## *My Locker Room Experience*

**Below is your chance to list areas of improvement you have as an athlete and as you huddle up with your teammates and coaches.** For example, attitude conflicts, lack of commitment, lackadaisical attitude, jealousy, and so on...

This book belongs to you so you do not have to hold back from being honest. No one has to read it but you. As you write these areas down, you should make sure that you strive to improve these areas to become a better person and athlete or coach.

COMMITMENT
IS IMPORTANT

Are you
committed?

To yourself?
The sport?
Your team?
Your Coach(s)?
Your Grades?
Why and how?

1. FAFSA- http://www.fafsa.ed.gov/
2. Kendrick Perkins:
    - http://espn.go.com/nba/player/_/id/2018/kendrick-perkins

    - http://en.wikipedia.org/wiki/Kendrick_Perkins

    - http://www.nba.com/playerfile/kendrick_perkins/

    - http://en.wikipedia.org/wiki/Kendrick_Perkins#High_school

    - http://www.beaumont.k12.tx.us/ozen/

3. YouTube, http://www.youtube.com/?tab=w1
4. SF Productions, www.sfproduction.net
5. Stephanie Franklin Ministries, www.stephaniefranklinministries.org
6. YouTube: SFMinistries
7. AAU: www.aausports.com
8. TAC: (USATF) www.usatf.org
9. YouTube: www.youtube.com
10. All scripture notations, unless otherwise indicated, are taken from The Holy Bible- King James version.2007.

**Check out Stephanie's nine books available for purchase on her website.** www.stephaniefranklinministries.org. You may also purchase them at Barnes & Noble, Books-A-Million, Amazon, and stores near you.

1       2       3       4       5       6       7       8       9

For more information on how to purchase Stephanie's books and paraphernalia, please visit www.stephaniefranklinministries.org or you may email: info@stephaniefranklinministries.org

**\*\*\*\*\*\*\*\*\*\*\*\*\*\*\*\*\*\*\*\*\*\*\*\*\*\*\*\***

**For information on how to purchase your Highlight Video, visit SF Productions Website at:** www.sfproduction.net **or you may email** sfproductions@sfproduction.net

**\*\*\*\*\*\*\*\*\*\*\*\*\*\*\*\*\*\*\*\*\*\*\*\*\*\*\*\***

*THE PURPOSE CENTER, Inc.* is committed to empowering youth and families to overcome challenges that may be a result of low-income neighborhoods and housing. It is dedicated to delivering real world solutions by understanding the real issues that affect the community. It has a genuine enthusiasm because it understands that the core of a community is the family. Strengthen the family, strengthen the community. The Purpose Center's goal is to act as a trusted extension of the community. It socially and academically educates, promotes health care and exercises and expresses the importance of family values. It's programs encourage community volunteering, teamwork and professionalism. It plans to work together to substantially increase the quality of life for the residents in this low-income area.

For more information on Purpose Center, Inc. email: thepurposecenter@ymail.com

*****************************

Stephanie Franklin Ministries has a mandated call to reach the world through teaching, preaching, mentoring, coaching, TV, CD, DVD, and books. Stephanie Franklin are called to present the Gospel of Jesus Christ to the lost, minister hope to the hopeless and healing to those that need to be healed.

For more information email: info@stephaniefranklinministries.com or you may visit: www.stephaniefranklinministries.org

# Stephanie Franklin, M Th.

is the author of, When Ramona Got Her Groove Back from God, My Song of Solomon, My Song of Solomon *Prayer Journal,* Position Your Faith for Great Success, Position Your Faith for Great Success *Workbook,* The Purpose Chaser: *For Children Ages 5 to 12,* God Loves Thugs Too!, and now her **two new releases**: Church Hurt: *How to Heal & Overcome It* and The Locker Room Experience: *For the Struggling Athlete & Coach, & Tips on How to Get Recruited in Sports.*

Stephanie has been an educator for over 15 years and in the coaching arena for over 20 years. Stephanie has a vision to reach the world with her mentoring, teaching, coaching and preaching ministry. She has a heart to reach the youth and young adults along with the entire family, bringing them all together as a unified fold.

She has received her Master of Arts Degree in Theological Studies and is on her way to pursuing her Doctrines Degree. Her mission while on this earth is to be used by God in whatever capacity He chooses.

She enjoys reading, writing, and spending time with family and friends.

*9781937911553*